SCHIRMER'S LIBRARY
OF MUSICAL CLASSICS

Vol. 2002

SERGEI RACHMANINOV

Etudes Tableaux, Op. 33
Nine Etudes Tableaux, Op. 39

For Piano

ISBN 978-0-7935-4518-6

G. SCHIRMER, Inc.

DISTRIBUTED BY

HAL•LEONARD®
CORPORATION
7777 W. BLUEMOUND RD. P.O. BOX 13819 MILWAUKEE, WI 53213

CONTENTS

ETUDES TABLEAUX

I

Sergei Rachmaninov, Op. 33

II

III[*]

* There were originally 9 Etudes Tableaux intended for Op. 32, three of which were withdrawn prior to publication.

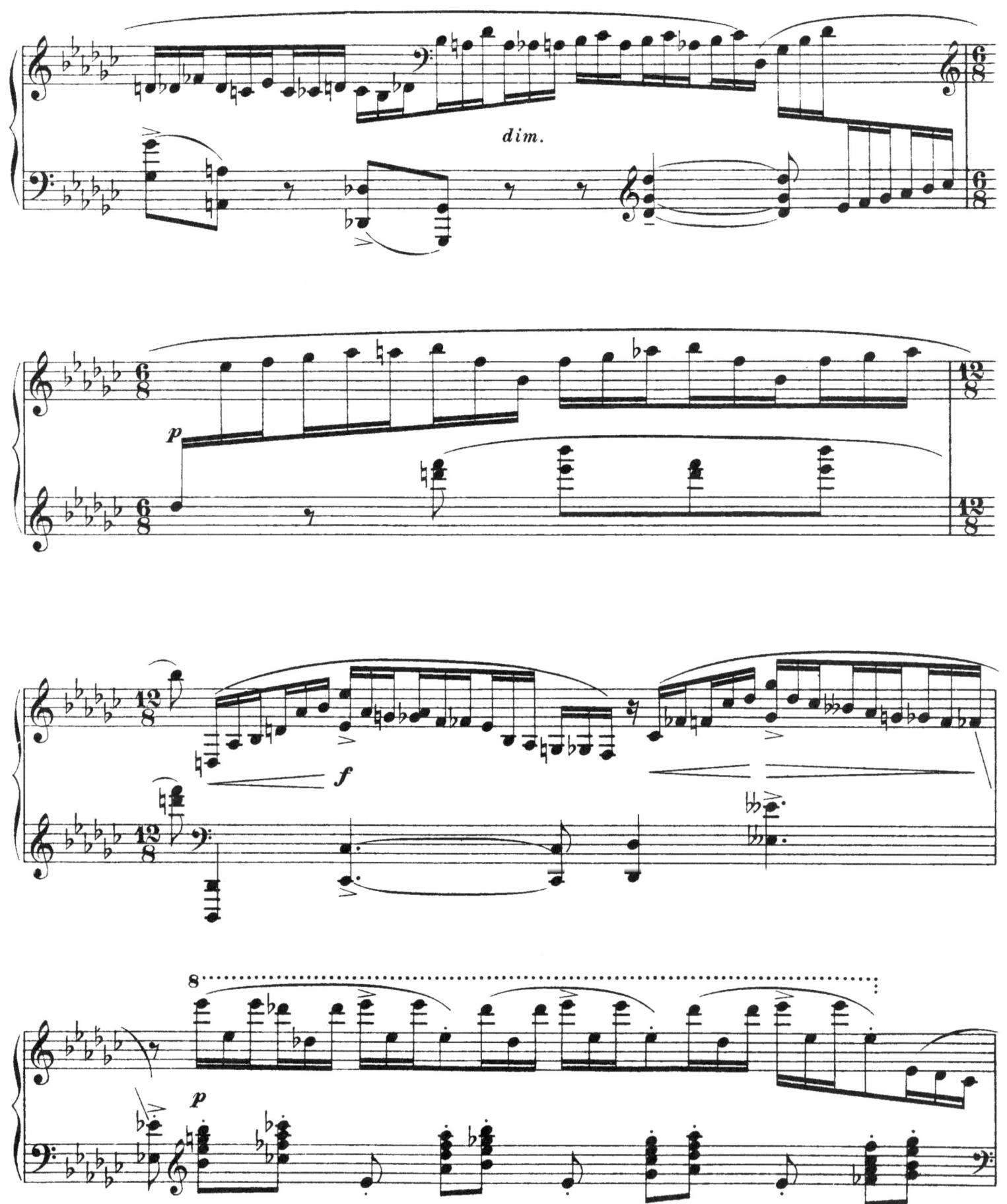

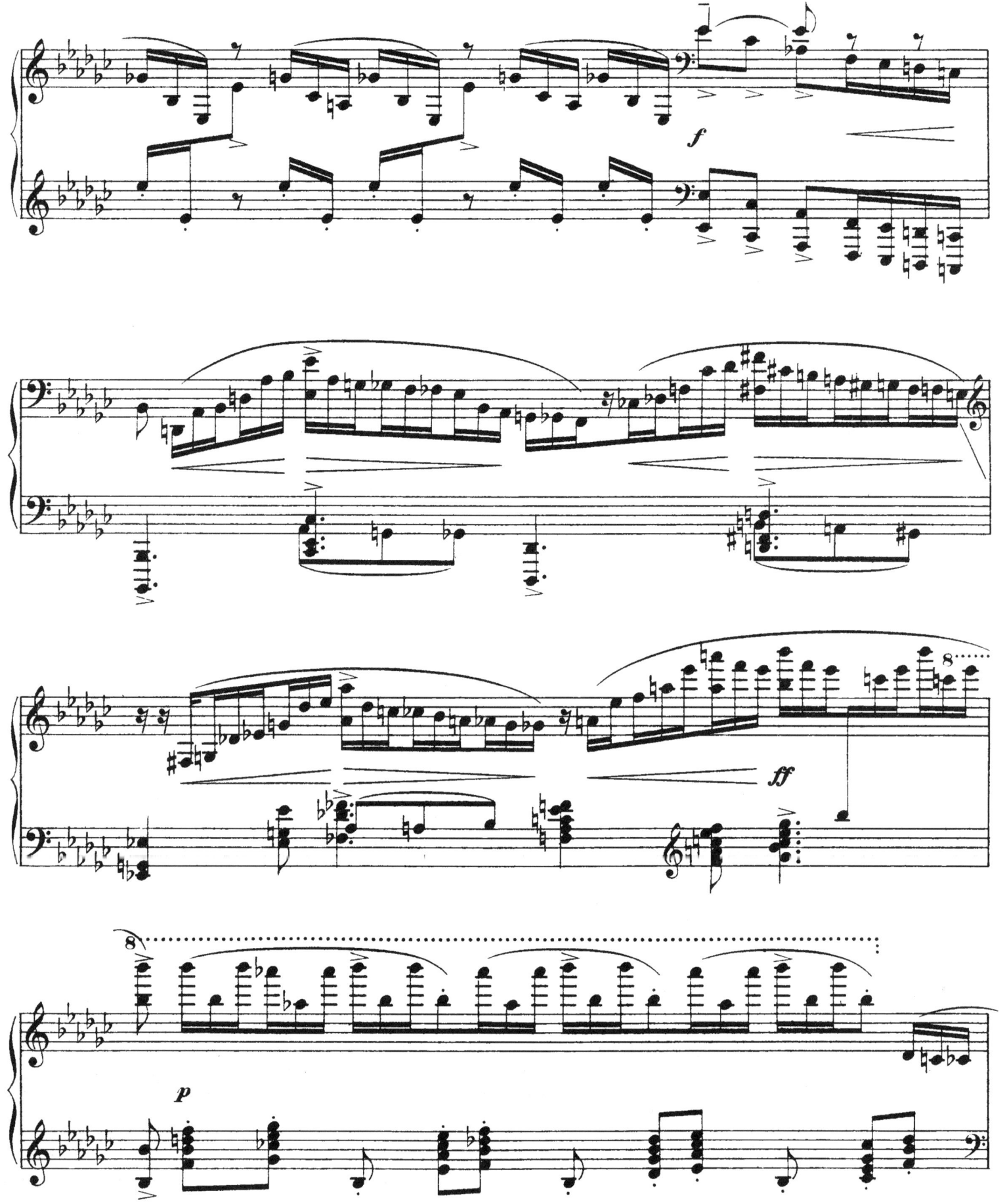

IV[*]

Allegro con fuoco

* Originally, No. 7

V*

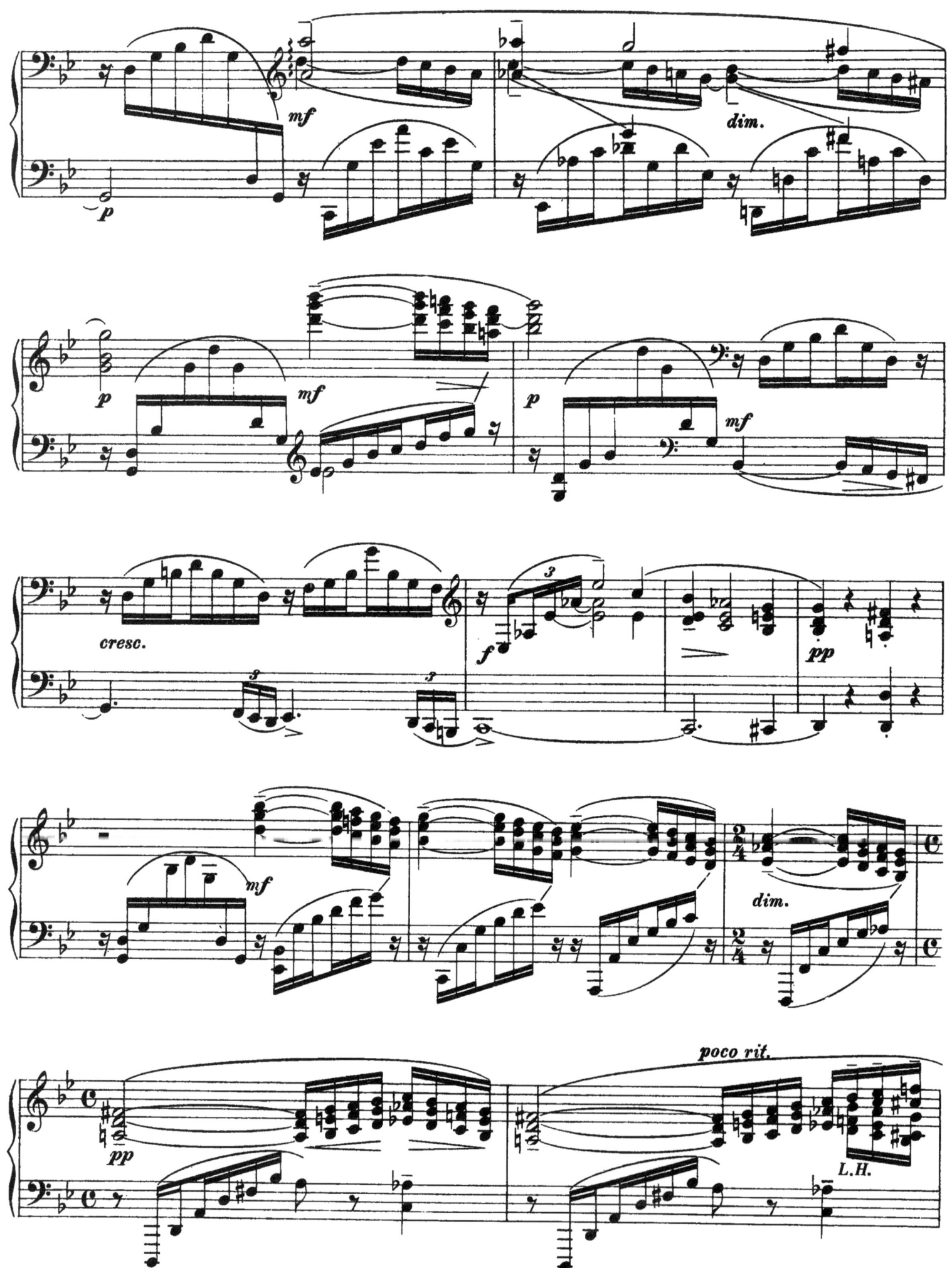

VI*

Tempo I

NINE ETUDES TABLEAUX

Op. 39

NINE ETUDES TABLEAUX

I

Sergei Rachmaninov, Op. 39

Allegro agitato

II

III

Allegro molto

IV

Allegro assai

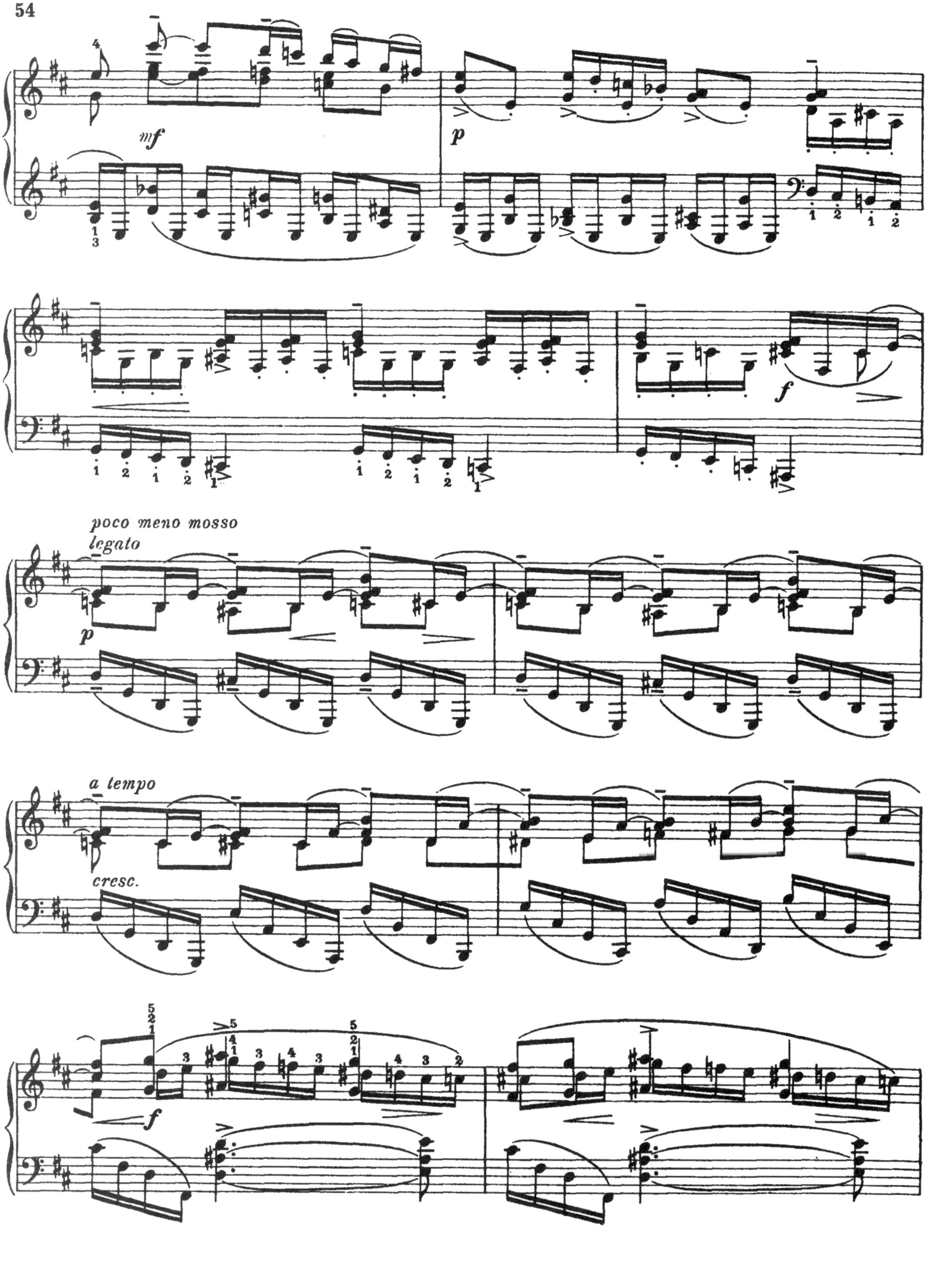
mf
p
f
poco meno mosso
legato
p
a tempo
cresc.
f

V

Apassionato
molto marcato

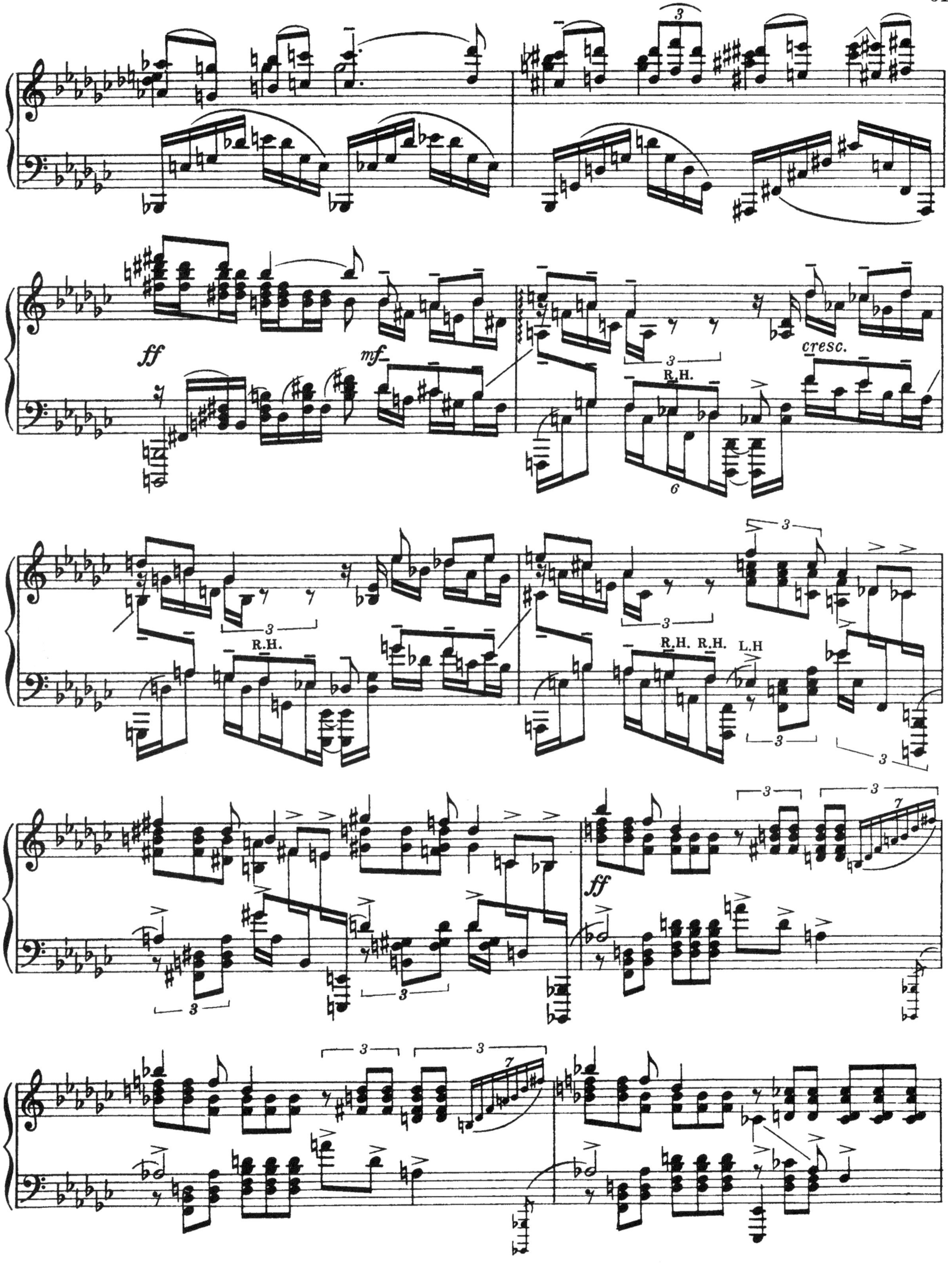
ff
mf
cresc.
R.H.
R.H.
R.H. R.H. L.H
ff

VI

Più mosso

Presto
leggiere

Tempo I

VII

VIII

IX

Allegro moderato Tempo di Marcia